Divali

LABURNUM PRESS

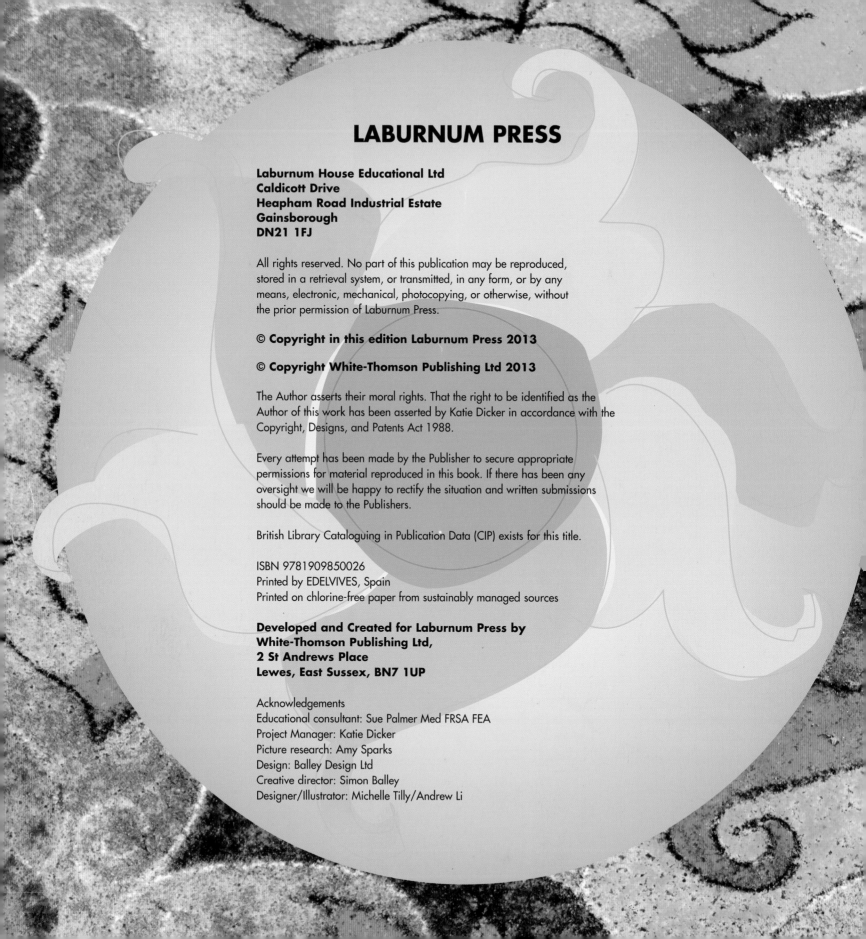

LABURNUM PRESS

Laburnum House Educational Ltd
Caldicott Drive
Heapham Road Industrial Estate
Gainsborough
DN21 1FJ

British Library Cataloguing in Publication Data (CIP) exists for this title.

ISBN 9781909850026
Printed by EDELVIVES, Spain
Printed on chlorine-free paper from sustainably managed sources

Developed and Created for Laburnum Press by
White-Thomson Publishing Ltd,
2 St Andrews Place
Lewes, East Sussex, BN7 1UP

Acknowledgements
Educational consultant: Sue Palmer Med FRSA FEA
Project Manager: Katie Dicker
Picture research: Amy Sparks
Design: Balley Design Ltd
Creative director: Simon Balley
Designer/Illustrator: Michelle Tilly/Andrew Li

Contents

Light up!

crackle!

bang!

It's Divali! This festival of lights is the start of the Hindu New Year.

4

People light candles, called divas, to celebrate.

warm glow

5

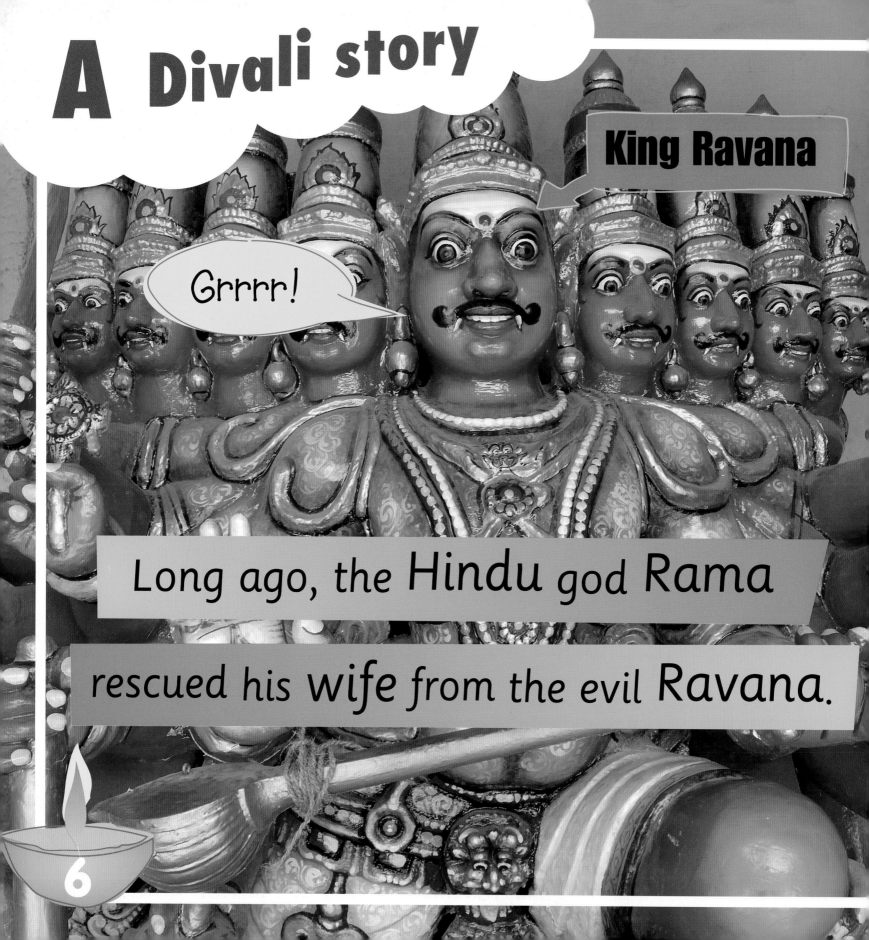

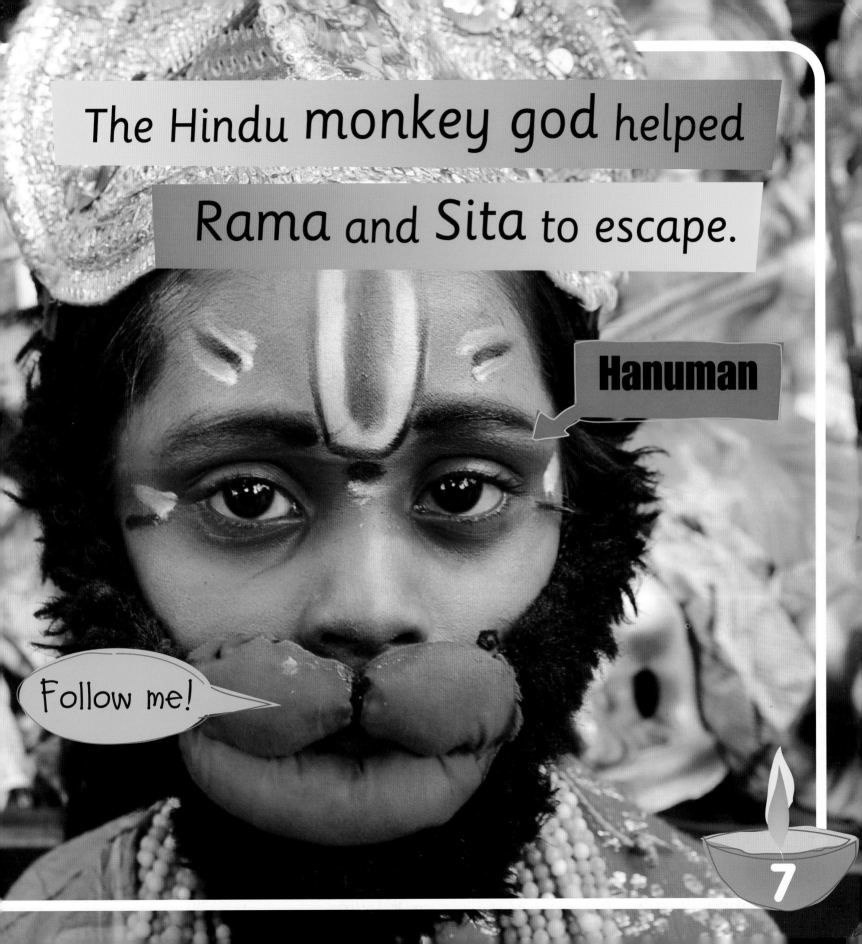

Today, we make **coloured** rice patterns to welcome the **gods** to our **homes.**

wiggle

9

What to wear

Special paints are used to decorate hands and feet.

matching pattern

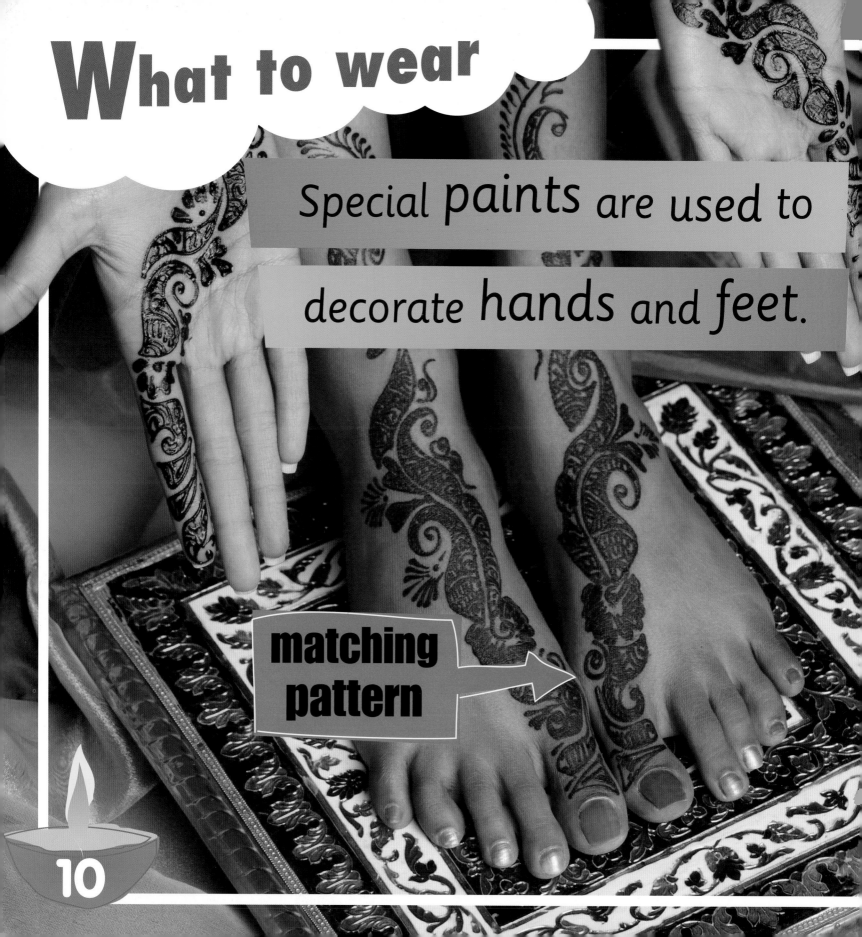

What **traditional** clothes

do YOU like to **wear?**

11

Happy New Year!

big hug

At the start of a new year, it's good to show your friendship to others.

12

Ganesh

long trunk

Hindus pray to the elephant god to wish them good luck!

13

Different traditions

Sikhs celebrate Divali with lights and candles, too.

Giving gifts

Thank you!

Divali is a time to give gifts to other people.

16

What would YOU use to make a Divali card?

sticky

17

Special feast

It's time to make a special meal.

This flat bread is called chapati.

squeeze!

18

Afterwards, we'll eat sweets made from coconut.

19

A celebration

glitter!

People have come to the temple for prayers and a party.

20

Swirl!

Help us to put on a Divali dance!

21

Notes for adults

Sparklers books are designed to support and extend the learning of young children. The **Food We Eat** titles won a Practical Pre-School Silver Award, the **Body Moves** titles won a Practical Pre-School Gold Award and the **Out and About** titles won the 2009 Practical Pre-School Gold Overall Winner Award. The books' high-interest subjects link in to the Early Years curriculum and beyond. Find out more about Early Years and reading with children from the National Literacy Trust (www.literacytrust.org.uk).

Themed titles
Divali is one of four **Celebrations** titles that encourage children to learn about annual festivals and different cultures around the world. The other titles are:

Christmas   **Easter**   **Chinese New Year**

Areas of learning
Each **Celebrations** title helps to support the following Early Years Foundation Stage areas of learning:
Personal, Social and Emotional Development
Communication, Language and Literacy
Problem Solving, Reasoning and Numeracy
Knowledge and Understanding of the World
Physical Development
Creative Development

Making the most of reading time
When reading with younger children, take time to explore the pictures together. Ask children to find, identify, count or describe different objects. Point out colours and textures. Allow quiet spaces in your reading so that children can ask questions or repeat your words. Try pausing mid-sentence so that children can predict the next word. This sort of participation develops early reading skills.

Follow the words with your finger as you read. The main text is in Infant Sassoon, a clear, friendly font designed for children learning to read and write. The labels and sound effects add fun and give the opportunity to distinguish between levels of communication. Where appropriate, labels, sound effects or main text may be presented phonically. Encourage children to imitate the sounds.

As you read the book, you can also take the opportunity to talk about the book itself with appropriate vocabulary such as "page", "cover", "back", "front", "photograph", "label" and "page number".

You can also extend children's learning by using the books as a springboard for discussion and further activities. There are a few suggestions on the facing page. The Internet also has many teaching resources about annual festivals. For example, see www.365celebration.com and www.underfives.co.uk.

Pages 4–5: Light up!

Talk to children about the difference between light and dark. What words can they think of that describe a change of light and the way it makes them feel? Children may enjoy making their own diva, or tea light holder, from play dough or clay. Use paint or varnish and decorate with colourful glitter. You could also talk to children about fireworks and the importance of fire safety.

Pages 6–7: A Divali story

Explain to children that the festival of Divali also celebrates the return of Rama and Sita in the Hindu story of the Ramayana. Use the Internet to help you (for example, www.hindunet.org/ramayana). Help to hone children's understanding with some activities, such as making and decorating masks or making shadow puppets of Rama, Sita, Ravana and Hanuman. How many heads and hands has Ravana got?

Pages 8–9: Divali decorations

Talk to children about the meaning of the words "Divali" (row of lights) and "rangoli" (row of colours). Help children to make their own decorations to bring light and colour to a room. You could make rangoli patterns by gluing coloured powder, sand, rice or glitter to black card. Or use a paper doily template with coloured paints. Explain to children that colours and lights are used to welcome the Hindu god Lakshmi, who brings wealth and good luck.

Pages 10–11: What to wear

What traditional clothes do the children like to wear for a celebration? Help girls to dress themselves in a sari or draw some mendhi (henna patterns) on card hand templates (for safety). Draw around the children's hands, cut out the card, and decorate with pens and paints or glitter and coloured sand. Children may also enjoy making necklaces or garlands from tubes of pasta or tissue paper flowers.

Pages 12–13: Happy New Year!

Explain to children that Divali is also the celebration of a new year. Encourage children to clean and tidy an area in preparation for a new start. What wishes would they like to make for the year ahead? What prayers would they say or write to the Hindu god Ganesh?

Pages 14–15: Different traditions

Explain to children that Sikhs also celebrate the power of light over dark and good over evil at Divali. Encourage children to talk about how their family celebrate Divali (or another festival). Organise a model boat (or diva) race on a small pool of water. Whose boat or candle reaches the other side first?

Pages 16–17: Giving gifts

Encourage children to make a Divali card wishing their friends or family a Happy New Year. Ask children to talk about who they would like to give a card to, and why. Divali is also a time to share food and clothes with those in need. Help children to wrap presents and make and write gift labels.

Pages 18–19: Special feast

Help children to make their own coconut sweets (or plain biscuits, if the children have a nut allergy). Ask children to prepare a table for a special meal. Encourage them to count as they lay the table – are there enough knives and forks to go round?

Pages 20–21: A celebration

Help children to put on their own Divali party. What clothes would they like to wear? What music do they like to listen to? Can the children dance to the sounds that they hear? You could also put on a traditional Divali dance. Use the Internet (such as www.youtube.com) for some demonstrations.

Index

Picture acknowledgements:
Corbis: cover boy (Athar Hussain/Reuters), 5 (Ken Seet), 9 (Bazuki Muhammad/Reuters), 10 (Vivek Sharma/Asia Images), 12 (Vivek Sharma/Asia Images), 13 (STR/epa), 14 (Ajay Verma/Reuters), 21 (Mark Bryan Makela/In Pictures);
Dreamstime: 2-3 rangoli (Karsten Koehler), 4 (Alexey Stiop), 8 (Nikhil Gangavane), 17 (Monika Adamczyk), 22-23 rangoli (Karsten Koehler), 24 rangoli (Karsten Koehler);
Getty Images: 7 (AFP), 15 (Martin Harvey), 20 (AFP); **IStockphoto:** cover stars (knickohr), 19 (High Views Designs); **Photolibrary:** 6 (V Muthuraman), 11 (Brand X Pictures), 18 (Radius Images); **Shutterstock:** 16 (Monkey Business Images).